10654132

FSVE   Oct 13
Canterbury   5.99
00021910

DONKEY TALES

DONKEY TALES

Dr Elisabeth D. Svendsen MBE

Whittet Books

First published 1995

© 1995 by Dr Elisabeth D. Svendsen M B E

Whittet Books Ltd, 18 Anley Road, London W14 OBY

The right of Elisabeth D Svendsen to be identified as the author of this work has been asserted in accordance with the Copyright , Designs and Patents Act 1988

British Library in Publication Data
A catalogue record for this book is available from the British Library

The Donkey Sanctuary is at Sidmouth, Devon. Tel no 01395 578222

Design by Richard Kelly

Drawings (pp. 13, 23, 26, 39, 46, 47, 51, 59, 73, 75, 83) by Tom Morse-Brown

ISBN 1 873580 22 3

The author and publishers are grateful to the following for permission to reproduce pictures on the pages indicated in brackets: Sonia Barry (60); Liz Bonfield (61); June Brown (72); Julie Courtney (89); June Evers (24, 32, 37, 40 bottom, 41, 57, 64 both, 68 all, 81); Pat Feather (90); Sandra Harrington (33, 44, 48, 54, 55, 63, 84, 93 all, 94); Molly Lloyd (71); David Mansell (87, 91); Tom Morse-Brown (pp. 11, 12, 14, 15, 17, 19, 20); Ray Mutter (53 left); Mary Pilkington (40 top); Marlene Reynolds (95 all, 96 bottom); Mal Squance (36, 69, 85); Shelagh Steele (21, 22); Alison Stephens (96 top); Paul Svendsen (endpaper, 53 right, 67, 76, 77, 79, 80); Bill Tetlow (28, 29, 31, 52, 88 all); Fritz Thewes (title page); *Sunday Independent* (56)

Printed in Hong Kong by South China Printing Co

Contents

*F*oreword

Since 1969, the world has been a better place for donkeys: that was when Elisabeth Svendsen founded the Donkey Sanctuary in Devon, a haven open to all donkeys; with a donkey hospital arguably better equipped than the NHS; the doors are open not only to donkeys in need, but also to their inseparable companion, be it pony, goat, pig or cow.

Elisabeth Svendsen is a dynamo of energy, who has used those energies to fight for donkeys in this country and around the world against hideous cruelty and exploitation. The Donkey Sanctuary has grown from one little stable to 9 farms; it has taken into its care 6,500 donkeys, and has sprouted other related charities to help handicapped children and to take the fight abroad. Mrs Svendsen has been awarded the MBE and an honorary doctorate of veterinary medicine and surgery.

The work of the Donkey Sanctuary ranges from taking up the cudgels on behalf of donkeys that have been ill treated (as you can read in the stories of Irish Thomas, Thirty-five donkeys in distress, Jingo got them on their knees and Cyril and Jack) to campaigning on issues such as better conditions for beach donkeys (about which you can read in Terence and Daisy) and to providing a safe haven for donkeys whose owners can no longer look after them.

The chance to stroke and love a gentle and cuddly donkey, and even the opportunity to learn to ride can prove beneficial therapy for children with special needs and disabilities; such gifts are provided by two related charities - the Slade Centre and the Elisabeth Svendsen Trust for Children and Donkeys. The Sanctuary chooses those donkeys suitable for giving children rides, thus providing pleasure for the children and a pleasant task for the donkeys. Tom Harrison, a model character whose story is told in the book, is one of those donkeys.

Surely it's tea time?

Annabel Whittet

7

Every One is Different

Many donkey characters arrive at the Sanctuary, and some make such an impression on different members of staff that they become almost immortal. They have some peculiar requirements too: their ex-owners say they will only eat Jaffa cakes, for instance, and one, Moko, had a passion for raw spinach! Simon liked brown bread, but it had to have a spoonful of sugar on, and many like a carrot at, say, 4 o'clock! We are always very careful to try and comply with the varying requests in an effort to reduce the stress felt by donkeys already in unfamiliar surroundings, but we were pretty hard pressed when told that Gary from Scotland liked the bagpipes being played to him! Whilst he was in our holding station up north, Frank Hindle, our Welfare Officer, managed to oblige, but I am afraid this was one request we couldn't fulfil here.

When Jeffrey came in, his ex-owner explained how he loved to share a gin and tonic, and had a very special trick she would like us to continue doing with him. To the delight of the staff, when asked,'What does Esther Rantzen do?' Jeffrey throws his head back and draws his lips back to show all his teeth!

Obviously some have tricks we have not been warned about. Two little donkeys, Winnie and Pooh, came in and, unfortunately, Winnie needed an X-ray. As you know, we never split friends up, and so they were both taken over to the hospital together. Pooh watched the proceedings with great interest, and Winnie was quite happy to stand still, knowing her friend was still in sight. As it was coffee time, the vet nurse assisting the veterinary surgeon put her coffee mug on the table behind her. A few moments later, hearing a clinking sound, she turned round to find her mug firmly clamped in Pooh's jaws, and Pooh, with his head tipped back, was happily swallowing the last drop!

Some of our worst cases have come in from people such as owners of public houses who have kept a stallion in their grounds and who have taken delight in giving them a glass of beer or lager, which donkeys can be trained to enjoy without too much effort. It is sad to see how many alcoholic donkeys we get in. Although rather amusing, no doubt, for publicans and their clientele to watch a donkey clamp its lips round a dimpled glass pint mug and swill it down in one go, it's a very different matter when the donkey gets aggressive and has to be sent to us for 'drying out'. Drying out, really, is exactly what it means; we have to treat them extremely carefully because, once addicted to beer and having become alcoholics, they show the same symptoms as humans when we have to start weaning them off their daily intake. This has to be done really slowly, starting with a pint of beer for the first few days whilst they get used to their new surroundings, and then gradually adding lemonade or water and reducing it to a shandy, and from thereon, very gently replacing it with a glass of lemonade or water. Nearly all the donkeys that have been alcoholics seem to find their way to Brookfield Farm once they have dried out, and then it's up to the other donkeys to sort them out.

Dribbling up the yard.

I think all the donkeys have heard of Brookfield Farm, which is where the 'Big Boys' group is situated. After donkey stallions have been castrated it takes them quite a while to lose their stallion tendencies and anyone who gets very difficult goes out to Brookfield Farm where the other donkeys in the group soon sort out any donkey with ideas above his station. It's surprising how often a small donkey becomes the 'boss' of any one unit – definitely not necessarily the biggest; surprisingly enough, many of the larger donkeys are the most gentle.

Many donkeys have learned tricks from their past owners, and trying to re-train them is difficult. Recently two donkeys came in who have caused more than their fair share of chaos: the first was Bambi Bishop. She came in on November 25th, 1994, having been living with another donkey which, sadly, had died; Bambi had become very lonely. Her owner felt that Bambi should be living a full and happy life with other donkeys, and was pleased when we paired Bambi with another donkey to be rehabilitated into another kind and loving home.

Bambi's original owner had two large dogs and apparently

Bambi's favourite game was football. She would play with the dogs for hours; picking up the football in her teeth, she would trot off with the dogs following closely behind. If the dogs got tired of the game, Bambi would look around; if they weren't there she would take the ball back to them and set off again. When it was time to go into the stables the owner would hold out her arms and say, 'Sleep, Bambi, come sleepy,' and Bambi would put her head on her owner's shoulder and lean on her until she nearly dropped off to sleep.

Whilst we had been given plenty of advice about the ball game with the dogs, Bambi's owner hadn't warned us about her skills

Bambi likes a shoulder to lean on.

in opening doors and it took her no time at all to discover how to draw back the little bolt of her stable door. All animals have to go into the isolation unit upon arrival; this special unit is run by highly trained, caring staff under the direct supervision of our veterinary department. The isolation staff spent the first few days trying to make the door 'Bambi-proof' as time and again she let out her little group of donkeys and of course they all went straight to the feed store, where they managed to snatch a few mouthfuls of food before the staff caught up with them. After a period of time in the isolation unit, Bambi was taken to our new rehabilitation/training centre at Paccombe Farm. This unit is where donkeys that seem suitable for re-homing are gathered together. Obviously we have to be terribly fussy where the donkeys go; prospective owners often say the procedure for adopting a donkey is harder than that for adopting a child. To me this is as it should be, because as a child grows older it can at least make a complaint, whereas a donkey can't and, hopefully, it will be in its new home for the rest of its natural life.

New owners are vetted very carefully: they must have adequate land, stabling and fencing and, most important of all, the knowledge necessary to look after the donkeys. The Sanctuary now runs training courses throughout the country and

Barnaby couldn't get into the stable *(see p.16)*

those wishing to give homes to donkeys are required to spend a day at our training centre, learning how to cope with the donkeys – which is for the good of both donkey and owner. Once the donkeys have been selected for their new homes, our Welfare Officer tries to be there when they arrive, to help to settle the donkeys in and answer any questions the new owner may have. The donkeys are then visited every three months in the first year, and every four months thereafter or, of course, on request if the new owner wishes.

I have always been a great believer in basic training and teaching people practically in a 'hands-on' manner. I shall never forget the experience of a very unhappy team of an international health organization that my colleague June Evers and I heard of while in Kenya. As you know, there are many cases of malaria in that part of Africa and in particular some isolated small villages reported very high numbers of cases with children frequently dying. This extremely well equipped team decided to visit these villages to warn the local people of the dangers of catching malaria and to offer free help and advice. When they arrived at the first village they met the local head man, who agreed to translate for them as many of the local people spoke only Swahili. They set up their projector screen and at the side of a clearing in the village they stood a table on which were free anti-malaria tablets, special pills which would stop the development of mosquito larvae in the stagnant water around the village, and sprays which would prevent the mosquitoes from biting in the first place. There was great excitement in the village, as they had never actually seen a film show of any sort before. Almost every member of the village attended and sat on the ground waiting in eager anticipation for the film. The head of the team explained that they were there because of the large number of cases of malaria and sickness in the village; this was translated by the head man and met with great approval and much nodding of heads. He then went on to explain that he would show them the

Barnaby's favourite trick (see p. 18).

Barnaby and friends.

cause of the problem, and showed a film featuring the mosquito (enlarged, of course, so that everyone could see it) and pointing out how the proboscis of the mosquito entered the skin as well as the larvae in the pools which would develop into full grown mosquitoes.

Having finished the film he then explained that their charity would supply free of charge medicines which would prevent them being bitten, which would help them when they had the bad fever, and medicines which they could put in their stagnant water to prevent the larvae. This was duly translated by the head man; then, to the team's absolute horror, all the people melted away, apart from a few little boys who stood looking at the table with some interest.

'But why have they all gone?' asked the leader. 'Why aren't they taking the free malaria drugs we are offering?'

The head man smiled at him very sweetly and said, 'Well, yes, we know the people are very ill here, and often the children die, but, you see, we don't get a problem from these mosquitoes.'

'But you do!' exclaimed the leader, smacking at a mosquito sitting on his arm. 'This is a mosquito.'

'Oh no,' the head man said, 'the ones you showed us on the film are much, much bigger. We don't get any like that here at all. We don't have that problem!'

This illustrates more than anything that you have to start with the basics in life and not assume that an audience to whom you are speaking is aware of all modern equipment and developments – even magnification on a cinema screen.

However, to return to Bambi Bishop, she went through her training period, during which time she was teamed up with a very sweet little donkey called Sammy. Unfortunately over the previous few weeks Bambi had reverted to many of her little tricks. No door seemed to be safe in the training centre and large chunks of wood seemed to be vanishing from many of the specially treated fences, which are supposed to be 'donkey-proof'. Bambi also appeared to be getting rather pushy; now she felt secure at the Sanctuary, certain bullying tactics were beginning to appear. When the prospective new rehab owner arrived to meet Bambi and Sammy to see if she would like the two donkeys, I'm afraid it was a disaster!

Bambi became even more aggressive and pushy with someone who wasn't quite sure how to handle donkeys, and Annie Chapman, who runs the department, had to rush in when Bambi had the rehab owner pinned against the wall of the training centre. Bambi, having decided suddenly to become sleepy, had put a very, very heavy head on the lady's shoulder and she was slowly sinking to the ground! It seems that Bambi has missed her chance of being rehabilitated and she will probably be sent to Three Gates Farm.

Barnaby came into the Sanctuary on December 20th, 1994, a short time after Bambi's arrival. He was purchased by a lady who was increasingly concerned about Barnaby standing alone in a field with no chance of getting into a stable, as this was always occupied by a very large horse. She approached the owner several times offering whatever price he wanted if he would sell Barnaby, but apparently he refused, saying he wanted to keep the donkey a little longer. Late one evening we received

*Muffin looking for a
treat (see p. 18).*

a very distraught telephone call from the lady saying that she
was moving house and if she did manage to buy the donkey,
would we pick him up urgently, as she was leaving the following day? She phoned again later that night to confirm that she
had indeed managed to purchase the donkey, and asked if we
could collect him at 10 a.m. the following morning. Our lorry
driver managed to make it in time, despite a difficult access
along a very muddy track and, as our two Welfare Officers, Peter and Valerie Scammell, said, 'It was really quite chaotic
loading him!'

Whilst Barnaby, on the whole, is a very nice little gelding, he
also has a trick which he seems totally unable to forget. He has

a habit of picking up buckets; he carries the bucket around his shelter banging it against every possible object, and then he trots quietly to the door and drops it outside into the yard. I don't think anyone minds empty buckets clattering over the door, but once Barnaby has eaten his own breakfast he is certainly not averse to going round and finding one of the older donkeys who is quietly enjoying his leisurely breakfast, only to find it snatched away by Barnaby who promptly trots to the door and drops it outside. Just recently he attempted to pick up a water trough, but fortunately this proved far too heavy for him, although the staff are quite convinced that the indents around the rim exactly match Barnaby's teeth.

Perhaps Barnaby is destined for the 'Big Boys' group! At this moment I'm not sure where he will go, but I have a feeling that he could well be sent to Brookfield Farm!

Another real character has been with us a long time. Muffin came into the Sanctuary in 1989 with quite severe breathing problems. He had a little friend called Rosalind but unfortunately she died shortly after her arrival. Muffin had been most unfortunate, having already had two major operations for sarcoids. These are cancer-like growths which appear on many donkeys and we have a 'sarcoid group' here for those donkeys we have to watch very carefully. There are various methods with which to treat sarcoids: either radical surgery or cryosurgery, by short-wave diathermy or by immunology. As with humans, once these growths begin to appear they tend to recur, and normally the sarcoid group is kept together. However, as well as having sarcoids, Muffin also had a lot of other problems.

As Muffin's previous owner said, 'He came to us with either bites or sores on him, and was rather bad-tempered. He has had sweet-itch and laminitis, for which we have treated him homeopathically, and he has responded well. Muffin later developed a sarcoid, which was operated on in the stable by our local vet, who had a job to build him up afterwards. About six years ago Muffin became ill, and the vet thought it was due to poisoning. Muffin was partly paralysed down one side for a few days, staggering and dragging his feet. The vet felt that his nervous system had been attacked. Within the last four years Muffin developed another growth, and as our vet doesn't use the 'freezing' method, he recommended other vets, where Muf-

*Are they bringing in
more hay?*

fin went for an operation. In fact five growths were found and removed. Although rather shocked from the operation, he recovered more quickly than before and, again, we managed to get rid of this problem. Now Muffin has developed COPD (chronic obstructive pulmonary disease). We have therefore tried washing the hay and he is on ventipulmin; he still continues coughing and is only free from this when we change to horsehage. He is also bedded on wood shavings and is beginning to put on weight, but the cost of feed alone has gone up from £2 per week to £16. In temperament Muffin has improved greatly, although he has a wicked sense of humour.'

The owner's letter ended with the interesting information that both Muffin and Rosalind had starred with Ronnie Barker in his last series of 'Clarence'. Although Ros was the main star, Muffin, off stage, was very much in the limelight. Due to his sense of humour, and generally showing off to much laughter, he finally bit Ronnie Barker!

Also on his intake sheet were two comments: 1. loves peppermints and carrots, and 2. hates vets and blacksmiths. How right this is!

Because of his illnesses, Muffin was not kept in the sarcoid group, but moved to a unit in what we call 'Buffalo Barn'. This is a large, airy barn which has specially treated dust-free straw on the ground, and the donkeys are given dust-free hay. Many donkeys with bronchial problems are in this group, but –

I'll soon sort this out.

surprise, surprise – the donkey in charge of this unit is Muffin. He has completely taken control, and every morning as John Rabjohns and his team unload the bales of hay and put them into the feeders, no donkey dares to go near until Muffin has examined it thoroughly. If he finds the hay is not to his satisfaction, then he turns round and kicks the bale soundly. He has even been known to put his front hooves on the shoulders of the man delivering the hay to show extreme disapproval! The staff are now very wary of Muffin when going in and I can assure you that only the best hay ever goes to Buffalo Barn.

During the summer Muffin again proves he is the boss. As you possibly know, to protect the grass and to ensure that the donkeys always have fresh clean grass every day we use a system of electric fencing. This enables the donkeys to use approximately one quarter of a field per day, which gives them plenty of room to move around and plenty of fresh grass. The electric fencing is moved to its new position by the staff first thing in the morning. Once again, Muffin is always standing and checking very carefully how far the fence is being moved and the quality of the grass the donkeys will be eating that day.

Muffin really is a character, and very much loved by all the staff. If you were to go into the Buffalo Barn group when you visit, I can guarantee that the first donkey to come and give you a welcome would be Muffin – providing you are carrying sweet hay!

Jingo Got Them on Their Knees

Although, thankfully, there are not too many cases of direct cruelty to donkeys in the UK, they can get into serious trouble by being 'turned away' in the winter. Donkeys are not indigenous to this country; they much prefer the drier heat found in other countries. The coat of the donkey is not waterproof and can soon become sodden, causing great discomfort to the donkey and the very real threat of pneumonia should the weather turn extremely cold. For this reason a group of animal lovers from Frinton and Walton-on-the-Naze, led by Pamela Garrad, were concerned to find a donkey having to winter out on Holland marshes. Not only did the donkey have no shelter or food provided, but she had to compete with 43 horses for the poor grazing that was available. As the weather grew worse and snow began to fall, the group became more and more concerned for the donkey's welfare, and together they managed to raise

Holland marshes.

Jingo before being rescued.

enough money to buy her and remove her from the terrible conditions. They named her Jingo, and immediately contacted our Donkey Sanctuary representative, Shelagh Steel, who lives in Essex. Realizing the seriousness of the problems, Shelagh immediately arranged to go over with her trailer to pick Jingo up and move her to the warmth and safety of her stables.

When Shelagh arrived at the marsh she was horrified to find several policemen with barricades on the roads, and to hear that the ponies and donkey had between them broken down the gate onto the road and, just prior to Shelagh's arrival, there had been a panic round-up of the desperate group. When Shelagh managed to single Jingo out from the horses, and with the help of those present had loaded the poor, shivering donkey onto the trailer, she realized how extreme Jingo's plight was.

Quickly driving Jingo back to her holding station at her home, Shelagh unloaded the donkey, who was so terrified that she immediately retreated to the back of the stable and Shelagh was unable to get anywhere near her. She left Jingo to get used to her surroundings for some time and to enjoy the warmth and comfort of a stable for the first time and the hay and clean water available. After some time Shelagh approached her with a small feed. As with humans, when a donkey has gone through a starvation period for a long time, feeding has to be started very slowly, otherwise the donkey can suffer acute colic. To her horror, Shelagh found that the only way she could get within reach of the donkey was to crawl on her hands and knees. Very carefully she was able to put a bucket where Jingo could eagerly begin her first feed for a very long time.

Shelagh was absolutely appalled at the state of Jingo; she was frozen and shivering, and, running her hands through the donkey's coat, Shelagh could feel hard scars, probably the result of bites and kicks from other animals whilst on the marshes. Her feet were in a terrible state, as the marsh had begun to flood just before Jingo was rescued, and it was obvious that she needed immediate veterinary and farriery treatment.

As there was some possibility that Jingo could be in foal, it was decided to move her to the Donkey Sanctuary as soon as possible. It was a delighted Mrs Garrad who called to see Jingo just before she was brought to Devon; she was so pleased to see her rescued friend now safe and warm and obviously on the road to recovery. Although Mrs Garrad and her friends had paid £300 to get Jingo away from her owner, she felt it was worth every penny.

The Donkey Sanctuary's lorry, which is adapted to carry donkeys comfortably from all over the country, picked Jingo up on November 25th, 1994, and Jingo was brought carefully to the Sanctuary in Devon, where she was first put in the isolation unit, as are all donkeys on arrival.

Whatever the likes and dislikes of the donkey, during the six-

Shelagh trying to get Jingo's confidence.

Jingo happily settled with new friend Holly.

keep to the regime that the donkey was used to in the past. This alleviates to a large extent the trauma of losing their homes, and helps them adapt to the change without too much stress. The isolation unit is run by Ian Westlake, known to all as Wurzel. Wurzel has run his own farm and is well known locally, as he plays rugby for the local team and has a physique to match! He has worked for the Sanctuary for many years and, as usual, before the arrival of the lorry, he carefully studied the instructions from the Welfare Officer so that he and his colleagues could give Jingo the best attention on arrival. At that time, June Evers was caring for special donkeys, and June and Wurzel read Jingo's requirements. Obviously this donkey had not come from a loving home, and there were no notes such as 'requires Jaffa cakes or carrots' here. There was, however, one alarming comment from the Welfare Officer. This said, 'Always approach in a crawling position, otherwise this donkey will be terrified.' Wurzel and June looked at each other with some concern; the thought of Wurzel crawling towards the donkey really stretched everyone's imaginations! However, they realized that every possible care had to be taken to settle this little donkey in.

The lorry duly arrived, and with great care Brian McConnell,

24

the driver, led Jingo off the lorry. Everyone stood back to look at Jingo, being careful not to frighten her in any way, and Brian gently led her into the stable which had been prepared. For Jingo it must have been like a miracle; perhaps when she was loaded onto the lorry she thought she was leaving her lovely stable and being taken back to the terrible conditions under which she had been living previously.

Jingo was quite obviously delighted with her new accommodation. As all donkeys do, she walked around, sniffing and checking where the water was, and then she went back to the door to look out. To her joy, she heard a bray of welcome from the other donkeys in the isolation unit. As she already had a feed, which had been put in the stable ready for arrival, the isolation staff decided not to trouble her any more that evening but to let her have a good rest until the following morning.

The next day there was a discussion in the staff room as to who was going to crawl on their hands and knees to feed Jingo that morning. To everyone's delight, Wurzel drew the short straw and all the staff gathered round with some amusement to see how he coped in this new method of approach. Whilst Wurzel has no objection to being bent double in a rugby scrum, there was no way he was going to crawl into Jingo's stable in front of the staff, and so very quietly and using all his stockman's intuition, he opened the door and quietly walked in. To everyone's amazement, Jingo immediately moved forward and welcomed him with a nuzzle of delight. Whatever had happened in the past to make Jingo so terrified was now just a dim memory, and from that moment Jingo was a changed donkey. She settled in very happily, and within three days had joined a group of donkeys, as the policy of the isolation unit is to get donkeys into small groups so that when they eventually go out into the main Sanctuary and are allocated to one of the farms, they go as a little unit, which helps them integrate more easily.

Jingo was selected to go to Three Gates Farm in Dorset, and, some weeks later, already putting on weight and happily settled, she was transferred to this beautiful farm, where she is now living a contented, peaceful life with her new friends.

*T*erence and *Daisy: a Fond Reunion*

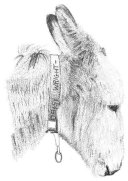

There are approximately 900 donkeys working on the beaches around the UK. For many years in the past these donkeys were made to work very long hours, often standing on the beaches from early in the morning until the sun went down at night. There were no laws to protect them and beach operators were free to mistreat the donkeys in order to further their own ends. When I first started rescuing donkeys I was appalled at the conditions on some of the beaches and on one occasion I almost got into physical trouble at Weston-super-Mare, where I was desperately concerned to see donkeys being urged to break into a trot or gallop by an operator using an electric goad, and even more concerned to find a small foal on the beach being used to draw the crowds. At this time only one council in the country seemed to operate any rules on its beaches, and this was Blackpool. They have been operating their Donkey Charter now for well over a hundred years and, with the odd exception, this had provided donkeys with a certain amount of protection during the working season.

Over the past three years the Sanctuary has been campaigning in a positive manner to raise the standards of the working beach donkeys. Although things today have very much improved, and to work on a beach the operator has to have a licence, there is still room for improvement. In particular we are very concerned at the plight of beach donkeys during the

Daisy and the lucky horseshoe charm.

winter. None of the regulations for work on the beach include adequate care for the donkeys out of season, and we are frequently called by concerned members of the public to donkeys having to spend the winter under dreadful conditions, and very often these donkeys have to be taken into care.

Most local government authorities require the donkeys that work on the beach to be licensed as this is a source of revenue for them (a licence for a stud of beach donkeys costs between £100 and £1,600 depending on the resort). All the operator has to do to acquire a licence is to show proof of a certificate of third party insurance and a veterinary certificate stating that the donkeys are fit for work. Unfortunately the policing of this tends to be very sloppy; often the veterinary certificate gets overlooked and even if one is produced there is no guarantee that the donkeys the vet had seen were the ones that ended up on the beach. Licensed operators can then use their donkeys on the beach according to the regulations laid down, which ensure the donkeys have adequate rest, water and feed, and that no goads or cruel aids are used during the rides. Over the last few years we have been promoting the use of hoof-branding. This causes no pain at all to the donkey but it ensures that when the inspection is carried out the donkeys actually inspected and passed as fit for work are those that are used on the beach. Our inspectors visiting on a regular basis can ensure that another donkey has not been substituted for the selected one. Obviously in the past the licensing system has been open to abuse; an operator could have eight donkeys passed for use on the beach, choosing the best of his stock; having got these passed, he could then exchange them for donkeys in a much poorer condition and sell on those for which he could get more money. It was seeing this happening again and again that motivated the Sanctuary into taking positive action. It campaigned actively to persuade local authorities to adopt some form of positive identification of the donkeys that had been passed fit at the veterinary inspection stage of the licensing so that only the fit and healthy donkeys ended up working on the beach. Hoof-branding has been a big step forward.

Blackpool was the first resort to show an interest, and after we spent many hours in consultation and attending council committee meetings they changed the local byelaws which made it

a legal requirement that all donkeys working on the beaches had to carry some form of identification. The Sanctuary offered through its farriery department to hoof-brand all the donkeys passed fit for work. This was quite an undertaking as there are over two hundred working donkeys on the beaches of Blackpool. The first donkeys were branded in 1991 and the Sanctuary has attended all the inspections since.

In 1994 Scarborough adopted the scheme and now all the donkeys working in Scarborough, Filey and Whitby are covered by this.

If the above is put into practice it should go a long way towards ensuring that a seaside resort can be proud of the donkeys

Beach donkeys having lunch at Scarborough.

Blackpool beach donkeys working.

working on the beach, and in return the donkeys can bring happiness to a small child's holiday with what may be his or her first contact with an animal of any species.

Many operators, however, are extremely concerned for their donkeys' welfare, and we receive donkeys for retirement to the Sanctuary when the operator thinks they have come to the end of their working lives. Two such donkeys were Terence and Daisy, both of whom came from Blackpool. The operator rang us and said she would like to retire Terence, who was then 25 years old, and she asked if we could take him into care. He had previously been in a group with three mares, three geldings and a colt. The operator was really concerned to ensure that Terence would have companions when he came to the Sanctuary, and that he would be kept by us for the rest of his natural life. On September 8th, 1993, our Regional Welfare Officer for Northern England, Bill Tetlow, collected Terence and took him to our holding base at Buxton as the first stage of his long journey to Sidmouth.

Although in an isolated area, Newton Farm near Buxton is a marvellous 'halfway house' for donkeys from the north travelling down to Devon. Newton Farm was originally called 'Bull i'th Thorn Farm' and the owner, who was an animal lover, had stated in his will that the farm was to be offered to a charity which his executors thought would make the most use of it for animal welfare. When the owner died, we were one of the charities to be given the chance to prove our need for such a farm, and I am very pleased indeed to say that we were selected to receive it. Although we loved the original name, we were asked to re-name it Newton Farm in memory of the previous owner. Having been renovated to enable it to take the maximum number of donkeys in the maximum comfort, the farm was officially opened on April 24th, 1992. We had a small ceremony to which we invited the solicitor who had handled the estate, together with the executors of the will, to meet the first of the long-eared inmates.

We offered the management of the farm to Ray Mutter, who had been working at the Sanctuary in Sidmouth for many years. He was at that time engaged to Julie Hussen, who worked in our veterinary department. Rather craftily we suggested that we would prefer a married couple to run the farm – the result of which was that Ray and Julie tied the knot and to this day are running Newton Farm most successfully.

Terence was duly given a few days to get over his journey and get used to his new regime, and then it was time for him to travel to Sidmouth and the isolation unit. Everyone was very amused to see that, round his neck, Terence wore a small collar on which a lucky brass horseshoe charm was hung, and there were strict instructions from the beach operator that Terence was to keep his lucky charm around his neck at all times. Whilst in the isolation unit he had the necessary inoculations to protect him from equine flu and tetanus, had his feet attended to, was wormed, and had a complete and thorough medical check.

Waiting for a ride.

After his six weeks in the isolation unit, where he began to get used to the group of donkeys he was with, Terence moved with them to the bigger Clifford Smith barn, where he was able to bond and integrate with a larger group of donkeys before the whole group was moved to Three Gates Farm. The group arrived there on December 10th, 1993.

My very first employee whilst I was still at the Salston Hotel and running my Donkey Sanctuary more as a hobby than as a full-time job was a wonderful man called Herb Fry. On moving to Slade House Farm his son, John, joined us with his wife, Monica. As the Sanctuary expanded, we purchased Three Gates Farm in Dorset, and John Fry seemed the ideal person to run this, as I knew I could rely on him entirely without constant supervision from the main farm. When his two sons, Peter and Tim, grew older they too joined the staff and, although Herb has now retired, the Fry family play a very active part in the day-to-day running of the Sanctuary. I was happy to find that,

between them, the Frys have given 76 years of service to the Donkey Sanctuary – not a bad record!

To return to Terence, he settled down fairly happily at Three Gates Farm, and the story continues with a call from the same beach operator with regard to another little donkey called Daisy. Daisy was 25 years old, and the operator felt it was time that this donkey too was retired and taken into care. Once again, Bill Tetlow collected the donkey and, after a few days rest at Newton Farm, Daisy arrived at the Donkey Sanctuary in Sidmouth on October 26th, 1994. As with Terence, Daisy arrived with a lucky brass horseshoe charm. The owner had been very clear in her request that, if possible, Daisy was to be reunited with Terence.

When I first met Daisy in the isolation unit I was puzzled to see that she was wearing a red collar. We identify all our donkeys with a special colour-coded collar: the mares wear yellow, the geldings wear red and the stallions who come in wear white, so that there is no chance that they can be mixed with any of the yellow-collar-wearers. The stallions are removed to the special stallion quarters adjacent to the veterinary department. I was very confused by Daisy's collar and, having given her a cuddle and told her what a good girl she was, I then found to my surprise that she was in fact a gelding! I do find it very difficult sometimes to equate the sex with the names given to donkeys; we also have Prince, who is a mare! We have to be very careful to check the sex of the donkeys coming in, as obviously errors in not spotting a stallion could have disastrous consequences with so many mares at the Sanctuary.

Daisy, having completed his period in the isolation unit, eventually arrived at Three Gates Farm with a small group of donkeys. For the first few days this group stayed in a small holding area on the edge of the farm, where in the distance they could see the large number of donkeys enjoying their freedom. During the winter months all the donkeys have to stay in because the fields become so waterlogged, and sharp little hooves would soon ensure that there was no nice spring grass for them later on. All the donkeys have beautiful large airy barns connected by concrete run-out yards and at Three Gates Farm the 680 donkeys have perhaps the largest area of any of our nine farms for over-wintering. It amounts to almost an acre in size and contains a number of really large barns with small cosy

Having a cuddle with Monica.

shelters for those donkeys who prefer more individual sleeping quarters. The donkeys are allowed to make their choice and move around freely with their friends, feeding and resting where they like.

On the day that Daisy and his group were to be introduced into the large unit, Monica Fry took a special interest, knowing the previous link between Terence and Daisy. A very long feeder was stretched right across the yard and Terence was happily eating with his friends when the new group was introduced. Probably purely by chance, Daisy walked to an empty space at the feeder opposite Terence, and for a few moments both donkeys concentrated on their food. Monica was watching, and she suddenly realized that Terence had stopped feeding and was staring at Daisy across the feeder. Daisy then looked up, and with no further ado, Terence immediately left his side and walked right round to stand close to Daisy. Monica just couldn't believe it, and must have called out, 'Terence, how lovely,' or something which she can't quite recall. Both donkeys turned round and began to walk towards her. Daisy was leading, and Monica confessed to having tears in her eyes as she saw Terence gently nuzzling at Daisy's neck as they walked together. It was such a lovely sight that Monica said, 'It really made my job worthwhile,' and it proves conclusively the enormous friendships donkeys make. Although they say an elephant never forgets, I think I would like to add that a donkey never forgets either.

Lesley Kicks up Her Heels

Without our excellent welfare force out in the field, many of the sad cases that come to us would not have been saved. This particular story relates to a group of fourteen donkeys who were owned by a very elderly lady of 97 who lived in Sussex. Through the grapevine our Welfare Officer, Shelagh Steel, had heard that there was a large group of donkeys in trouble and with very long feet, but she had not been given an address. Shelagh stepped up her efforts to try and find where they were, and eventually she managed to locate them. When she visited, she discovered that the owner had died the previous day. Although the donkeys were in the care of an elderly farm-hand, who in the past had trimmed the donkeys' hooves, he was now unable to do this following an accident when he had broken his big toe. It seemed that the donkeys had in fact been left to a grand-daughter and she was on her way to Sussex to see what could be done. Shelagh was quite appalled by the state of the donkeys. Without exception they were all very small and thin. As there were stallions running with the group it was apparent that some of the poor thin mares were already in foal. When Shelagh rang the Sanctuary to advise us of the situation it was agreed that if we could get the donkeys signed over to us, two of our specially designed and equipped lorries would be sent immediately, along with one of our veterinary nurses. Fortunately, on the grand-daughter's arrival, she promptly agreed that the donkeys should come to the Sanctuary, as she already had two donkeys of her own and felt she could not possibly cope with such a large group.

On April 13th our two drivers, Brian and Gerald, departed in the lorries, taking Dawn, the veterinary nurse, with them. We had already sent a farrier to trim all the donkeys' feet so that they were able to travel in reasonable comfort, but obviously a great deal more needed to be done to get the donkeys on the road to recovery. Both Gerald and Brian reported that the moment the donkeys were put onto the lorry they found the hay net and started eating. Our lorries travel very slowly and the drivers take special care to give the animals plenty of rest and to ensure that they are all getting food and water, in this case so much needed.

On arrival at the Sanctuary one little foal, Snowflake, who was very ill, was put into intensive care, but sadly he died soon afterwards. He was found to be totally riddled with worms. Of course, all those that had come in were wormed and the group were put into a large stable in the isolation unit where they could be specially treated, have intensive care, lots of cuddles, and gradually recover to full health.

The Sanctuary has to rely totally on voluntary donations and legacies, as we receive no government aid of any sort, and we were delighted when one of our loyal supporters sent us a generous donation to help with the cost of the large group we had taken in, and at the same time she asked if it was at all possible if we could name one of the foals Pankie. By coincidence just a few days later a beautiful little broken-coloured colt was born to a mare called Ruby, and so he was given this special name.

Another of the group was called Mary who was very small. Even after her feet had been treated, her hind feet were still twisted, making walking difficult for her. On her arrival at the Sanctuary it had seemed possible that she was in foal, although she was in such a poor condition generally that it was difficult to ascertain. Within two months it became obvious that she was pregnant, and everyone paid extra attention to her, as we felt she would probably have a difficult time producing her foal because she was so small. It was on Saturday afternoon, August 27th, that I received a desperate call from the isola-

RIGHT ABOVE Lesley looking for her mother.

RIGHT BELOW Lesley in splints with adopted grandmother Mary Pilkington

Ruby with Pankie at two days old.

36

tion unit to say that help was urgently needed. Along with June Evers, my colleague, who worked in the isolation unit, I ran across the road. There in the field, just behind the main shelter, lay a little brown foal, but where was the mother? Quickly looking round the donkeys we soon found Mary, and quietly led her back towards the little foal which she had abandoned. To our horror she showed absolutely no interest in the foal. I picked the little foal up in my arms and took it back to the stable, with June leading Mary behind me. While waiting for our veterinary surgeon to arrive to check that Mary had cleansed properly and to examine the little foal, we tried to get Mary to take some interest in the pathetic little creature I was holding. We tried everything; the foal seemed unable to stand and we helped it as best we could, thinking that if Mary saw it moving and approaching her, perhaps the maternal bond could be activated. But it was all to no avail. Our vet arrived and checked that both mother and baby were well, and we named the little foal Lesley after the vet's wife.

Thinking perhaps that Mary would feel happier outside rather than shut in the stable with little Lesley, we lifted Lesley up and took them both into a small paddock on their own. Poor little Lesley; she tried her hardest to suckle, but if she went anywhere near Mary she was in danger of receiving a blow from one of Mary's flying hooves. The poor thing staggered to a fence where the donkeys in the next paddock were showing great interest in her, but eventually we had to agree that a reconciliation was not going to take place that day, and with great difficulty we managed to take some milk from Mary which, of course, included the all-important colostrum (without which foals receive no immunity to many diseases) and we put this into a bottle with a special feed we keep for rejected foals, and Lesley had her first drink.

During the night Lesley and Mary were put into the stable, which was partitioned so that Lesley could reach across to her mother, but Mary couldn't go through to the other side, otherwise I'm quite sure we would have had a dead foal in the morning. We have 24-hour cover at the Sanctuary, and two night-watchmen patrol during the hours of darkness, and it seemed from the report the following morning that both of them had spent the majority of their time quietly watching Mary and

Off at 90 miles per hour.

Lesley's stable to see how they were getting on. The following morning we were all there early, hoping that Mary would change her mind and accept Lesley as her daughter. As the hours went by it became obvious that we were not going to succeed, certainly in getting the mother to feed the foal, although Mary did eventually soften and instead of kicking out at Lesley, she began to let her stand by her side. As the days went by Mary became more and more fond of Lesley, although she still would not allow her to come anywhere near her udder.

Feeding baby donkeys is a very time-consuming occupation. Fresh bottles have to be made up, and during the day Lesley was being fed every two hours, with three-hourly feeds during the night. Despite this she didn't seem to grow, and after a few weeks we realized that both her back legs were going to be severely deformed unless some urgent remedial treatment was carried out.

Poor Lesley; she ended up having plaster casts on each of her back legs in the hope that they would straighten and that later on she would be able to cavort and gallop like other donkey foals. Her mother Mary had been named after one of our 'ten yearers', that is one of our supporters who had attended our Donkey Week every year for ten years and who was allowed to

Siesta time.

A cuddle from Mum.

Resting near Mary.

have a donkey named after them. Lesley's mother had been named after Mary Pilkington. Mary and her husband have been attending Donkey Week for 'donkeys years' and Bill had already had a foal named after him. Now I had the great pleasure of writing to Mary to tell her that she had become a grandmother! We took some lovely pictures of Mary chatting to her 'grand-child' when she visited shortly after Lesley's plaster casts had been put on. These are pictures which Mary treasures highly.

Time has passed now and I am pleased to say that Lesley's legs have straightened. She still, however, has a problem in putting weight on. Part of the problem is, I think, that she is so energetic. During the winter the donkeys are in the warm barns; close to the isolation unit, where the donkeys need special exercise, small galloping fields are set aside. These are always well drained and during most of the winter they are reasonably dry. This special group of donkeys was allowed access to this land, and the problem with Lesley was that immediately the stable doors were opened, despite desperate brays from Mary, she would be off at 90 miles an hour galloping around the field time and time again, her head thrown up with delight, her tail streaming out behind and her little legs thundering over the turf.

Wurzel soon realized that this was the main cause of the problems with Lesley's weight; she used up so much energy on her gallops that there was little left over for her own nourishment! So her galloping time has had to be curtailed.

The whole group of donkeys has been kept in a special intensive care unit since its arrival, and at this moment I really feel they are going to need another twelve months before they are fit to go out as a group onto one of the farms. Each donkey has its own problems; some were starved so early in life that a constant veterinary watch is required to ensure that they get sufficient vitamins, extra feed and special farriery attention to undo their very bad start in life. Too many of the mares from this group have had foals far too young, and this not only drains the mares but, as in Lesley's case, takes its toll on the youngsters.

To enable the 'special care' donkeys to get extra exercise, many of them wear special 'donkey rugs' to withstand being outside in cold weather. The money for the rugs is donated by members of the public. Sometimes a waterproof rug is sufficient, but in the case of these donkeys, every single one has to have a special warm blanket underneath, as they are still too thin to cope with the cold weather. In addition to these warm rugs, which have to be removed when they come into the stables at night, they are all given the opportunity of standing under infra-red lamps and they are all fed on dust-free hay as, once again, there is a very real danger that their lungs were damaged before their rescue, and dusty hay is one of the main causes of irritation and respiratory disease in donkeys.

These donkeys will remain at the Donkey Sanctuary for the rest of their lives. We do not feel that any of them will ever be suitable for our rehabilitation scheme, and because the group has been together for so long, it would be unkind and unfair to split them up in the future. Hopefully their health will continue to improve and one day they will be fit enough to be transferred to one of our lovely farms where they will have not only beautiful warm barns to winter in but also hundreds of acres of rolling green Devonshire fields to gallop in.

Dinky, the 6,000th Donkey

I thought we should celebrate the arrival of our 6,000th donkey, although I wasn't sure whether it should be a celebration or a wake, if you know what I mean!

By chance, Dinky had a rather good story to tell. He is one of many donkeys who have come in not as a result of direct cruelty or neglect, but because of a change in the circumstances of his owner, who was going to live abroad. Shortly before Dinky was due to arrive I rang his owner, Mrs Gray, to tell her that Dinky was to be the 6,000th. Mrs Gray seemed over the moon that he was going to be such a celebrity, and wrote the most delightful letter back. I think the best way to tell you about Dinky is to print her letter:

'Dear Dr Svendsen

'I was delighted to receive your telephone call this morning about Dinky being the 6,000th donkey coming to the Donkey Sanctuary – it made the parting more of a celebration than a sad parting – and I know he will love the celebrity status – in his own quiet way!

'My husband bought me my first donkey as a birthday surprise when we lived at Durham – I thought I was getting a washing machine! Her name was Patsy, a gentle grey, but she was obviously lonely even though she was free to roam anywhere around the three acres surrounding the ruined house we were renovating and spent most of her time standing at the front door staring in, or glued to the kitchen window. So we asked around for a companion and a nearby farmer friend said that

43

Dinky and Miner arriving.

he had been landed with a donkey by a horse dealer and would be glad to be rid of it as it was chasing his cattle. This was Dinky, and although the farmer said we could have him, he wouldn't actually sell him to us as he was their family pet. We kept him for two years until one day the man called and said he needed some money to buy a horse and would we like to buy Dinky. Of course we said yes and paid quite a large price for those days (1969) of £50 because he knew we wouldn't part with him!

'All the years we lived at Durham, about five, Dinky always made an appearance in a pen in the picturesque market place in Durham at Christmas time as part of a Christmas tableau organized by the Lions – the farmer was a member, and when we went to see him he used to studiously ignore us because he was eating the highest quality hay which the man had for his trotters, and we only gave him second best!

'Dinky had a great time at Flass Hall with Patsy, with their own large stable block, and a couple of times he dislodged the catch of the door at the bottom of the extremely steep stairs going up to the hay loft, and having worked out that this was where the hay came from that was dropped down into the mangers, up he went – how I have never been able to imagine because you couldn't get steeper stairs! When I found him it then took four men to manhandle him back down – with extreme difficulty!

'We fenced off two large areas in the front "garden" for them, but pig netting was no match for Dinky and he persisted in crawling on his stomach under the netting – when you think how a piece of string will keep a pony in! – until we finally gave up and let them wander around the entire area. The trouble was we had to keep an eye on open doors as Dinky would be inside in a flash – Patsy was much too polite and would stand outside – and one day I caught him looking at himself in a long mirror which was temporarily propped up in the little sitting room, having come through the conservatory, down three steps, through the drawing room, through the large hall, up two steps, along a passage way and into the sitting room. As he is white I thought he was doing an advert for White Horse Whisky and I had had one too many when I saw him there!

'My two older children used to ride him a little, but taking him out for a walk was difficult because you had to have someone to also take Patsy as they wouldn't be parted. This proved most awkward one day when they had done an escape – Dinky could get around the end of our home-made cattle grid – and I couldn't find them anywhere. At last I went to a nearby farmer (who I'm afraid wasn't a great donkey-lover – I think they were too intelligent for him!) and he said he had shoved them in a field along the road. This was along a fairly main road and it was starting to become dusk. For some reason I can't recall I decided to walk them back one at a time and set off with Patsy. That was along the road, down the track and back over a little way to their field, which could be seen from the road. Then Dinky – well I got him equal to Patsy in the field and he would not move another inch, each calling madly to each other. It was now almost dark and I was absolutely stuck! I tried flagging cars down, but was ignored, until I accosted a cyclist, who kindly went to the house to ask my husband to bring Patsy to Dinky so that we could get them both back together!

Dinky looking in the mirror.

'They had a few lovely foals – one a broken-coloured one with white hooves – until I decided that although I might find loving homes for them, I couldn't guarantee that they would always have them, so birth control was brought in and Dinky was gelded.

'We moved to North Yorkshire where they had a horse for company, and when other horses were occasionally put in their field the horse would herd them into a corner and protect them with great vigour! Or if the horses chased the donkeys around, the donkeys would play along with them for a while then suddenly stop, kicking their heels up and the horses looked completely at a loss as to what to do next when they discovered the donkeys were not really bothered about them. Some horses are, of course, terrified of donkeys, and when we moved to Gloucestershire we were near to the Cirencester polo ground and somebody put their polo pony in the field next to the donkeys when they were out of sight around the side of the building. I appeared just in time to see this pony leaping a large wall, taking some of it with him, with fright on seeing the donkeys appearing. I then had to chase it round Cirencester Park for the next two hours! Stupid horse said the donkeys.

'After moving twice near Whitby where Dinky used to go down to the school bus to collect my daughter, they moved temporarily up to my brother-in-law's farm in Northumberland, then back down to Northallerton to some lovely fields next to a forest, but also deep, deep snow. Then down to near Gloucester where they lodged with another donkey along the road from where we lived. Unfortunately although the owner was very kind indeed to all the donkeys, his donkey was not at all nice and used to bite whenever he could, and with a two-year-old daughter, visits were a little fraught. We soon moved to Cirencester where they lived surrounded by hunters in the winter and polo ponies in the summer, and acted very superior! The family of little children who kept their ponies with us and my daughter, Helen, put on their own Nativity play in the magnificent Cotswold barn that we had – it was magical with Dinky playing a leading part and behaving impeccably (by this time Patsy had suddenly died with an undetected tumour in her intestines, but she certainly didn't betray any suffering or we would have noticed something was wrong – I do hope she didn't.)

'His constant companion for the last few years has been a miniature Shetland gelding aged 25, who originally came from Chatsworth and was then given to the Duchess's sister, Mrs

In the Christmas tableau.

Jackson, who lives nearby when he misbehaved in the Children's Corner! He is like a teddy bear and he and Dinky are great companions, and the third geriatric, also 25, is Helen's horse, a grey 15h gelding, which has gone to a lovely family for the mother to ride out with her daughter.

'I am so grateful to you for taking Dinky, and I will know that he will be looked after superbly and have other donkeys to talk to. Dinky loves to talk and he and I have shared many sorrows and triumphs over the years – he is such a good listener that I always know he understands! Just keep an eye on him as he doesn't "miss a trick" and quite often has dislodged the middle bar across their night time "stable" and squeezed over the bottom bar and under the top bar in order to get out just to show how clever he still is, and how stupid the ponies are because they can't do it!

'He and Patsy always used to know that I was away for a few days when we lived in North Yorks, and I would get my irate husband on the telephone saying he had been up since dawn chasing the donkeys around the village as they had somehow or other got out and gone walkabout! They never did it when I was there, and although a few shakes of some horse and pony

A big greeting for the celebrity.

nuts in a bucket and I could get them to do anything, they would ignore them when proffered by my husband!

'Happy days they have been with my donkeys, and I am very much looking forward to coming to see them at the Donkey Sanctuary. If we don't manage to get down before we go, which I hope we can, we shall certainly be with you in the summer when we come home for the holidays.

'I know everyone has lots of donkey stories to tell, but hopefully this will give some background to the proud 6,000th – he might be a little donkey with rather short ears and a pot belly (probably too much grass in the past), often chipped feet and sadly at the moment a bare patch down his face where the lice had been active (I never thought of them being active in this awful weather and they caught me out – so sorry) – but he is an enormous character and has always been loved very much.

'With endless thanks, yours sincerely

Elizabeth A Gray'

Knowing Dinky was travelling with his friend, Miner, who was said to be a rather difficult and naughty little Shetland pony, we all arranged to be at the isolation unit when they both arrived so that we could give them a proper welcome. They did look a most amusing pair, standing in the lorry, with Miner in fact being smaller than his donkey companion. They even hit the headlines in one of our local newspapers.

Following the excitement of their arrival, Dinky and Miner settled down very well indeed. We were able to write and reassure their owner that all was going well and that they had made friends with another little donkey and pony who had come in together called Charlie and Blue. We have been writing to Mrs Gray's mother, who lives in England, to keep everyone up to date with their progress. Dinky and Miner join me in wishing their ex-owners all happiness and success in their new life in Saudi Arabia.

Thirty-five Donkeys in Distress

I have seen many donkeys in distress in my lifetime, and have been moved to tears on more than one occasion, but I think the sight that met me when I was called to our holding base in Buxton in June 1993 was the worst I was ever to see. Thirty-five donkeys, some in foal, many emaciated, some covered in sores, all huddled together, frightened and dirty, and wondering what was going to happen to them next.

The rescue of these donkeys is to the credit of the RSPCA. We work with many other animal charities and have strong links with all those trying to improve conditions for donkeys. This story started on June 11th, 1993, when Bill Tetlow received a call from the RSPCA to say that they had taken a donkey into care as a result of a complaint. They asked if the Donkey Sanctuary could take the donkey in. Of course, we agreed; we have an agreement with the RSPCA that, if there is a problem, we will take the donkey into care immediately and provide evidence required by the RSPCA, who would bring any necessary prosecution. This seems to work very well: they have all the legal facilities available for court proceedings, and the Donkey Sanctuary has all the facilities available to look after the donkeys in trouble. In this case there was a great deal of concern about one particular donkey operator who was working his donkeys on Blackpool beach.

The RSPCA officer concerned was so worried by the state of one donkey on the beach that he called a veterinary surgeon, who immediately said the donkey must be removed from the beach. However, further investigation by the officer and the vet soon revealed that there were a further 15 donkeys at the beach who really were not fit to work. They insisted the whole group was removed and they were taken to a temporary home in Garstang. They were prepared to back up their decision with a written statement. Seeing the terrible state of these donkeys, the RSPCA officer asked their owner to see where the donkeys were kept, and he rang Bill Tetlow to warn that there were another 16 donkeys to be taken into care, and telling him that they were about to go and visit the donkeys' quarters. Bill asked if he could accompany them to the stables, and this was readily agreed. The donkeys were owned by a Mr Gardner, and when Bill arrived at Mr Gardner's stables at 3 o'clock in the afternoon he was absolutely horrified to find a dealer loading donkeys into a lorry. The donkeys were obviously in a very poor state and Bill advised the dealer that these donkeys should not be moved and should be left in the yard. Unfortunately no notice was taken of this advice and off went the lorry loaded with 8 terrified donkeys.

Bill jumped in his car and followed the vehicle, and telephoned the RSPCA en route. The RSPCA arrived and, with Bill, they stopped the vehicle and insisted that all the donkeys should be taken off as they were in such a terrible condition. They then returned to the stable yard, and met the veterinary surgeon. There were still 8 donkeys remaining in Mr Gardner's

The donkeys being loaded into the lorry.

Standing in solid donkey droppings.

stables and Bill, the RSPCA officer and the veterinary surgeon insisted that the donkeys must be removed because of the appalling state of the premises. They were standing in solid donkey droppings 18″ deep, covered in lice, their feet needing attention and looking like walking skeletons. Mr Gardner refused to allow the inspectors into every part of his property and eventually the police had to be called and some areas had to be broken into. To Bill's horror, 3 more donkeys were found locked up in a small room with the windows boarded. They were in a pitiful condition; covered in dung and obviously totally neglected and partially starved. The donkeys were so ill that none of them was fit to make a long journey but, with the vet's assistance, they were moved to the temporary home in Garstang, where they were able to spend six days being carefully fed and looked after before being moved to our holding base at Newton Farm. Unfortunately two donkeys were so sick that they had to stay in the private stables for a further three weeks before they were fit to travel.

It was a few days later, on June 17th, that I was able to see the donkeys for myself. We had been at Glasgow University where I had received my Honorary Doctorate, and it was there that we heard the news about these poor donkeys. We immediately set off for Newton Farm to see them for ourselves, and see what help we could give them. As I said earlier, it was the most hor-

Sara (left) *on arrival at the Sanctuary, and* (right) *six months later.*

rifying sight I have seen for years. It wasn't only that they were starving, had terrible injuries and long feet, but the fact that they were so terrified of humans was most distressing. Peter Ikin, the vet who had been with us in Glasgow, gave each donkey a medical examination, and one by one they received the loving attention they needed. They were put into comfortable stables, deeply bedded with straw, to start their return to the sort of life they had long forgotten. It was only after three weeks of intensive care, veterinary and farriery treatment, that the donkeys were able to travel the remainder of their journey to Sidmouth.

Our staff at the Sanctuary were equally distressed when the donkeys arrived, and it was obvious that it would be many months before they were able to join any particular group, as they needed constant supervision and care. As a prosecution was pending against Mr Gardner we kept very quiet about the arrival of these donkeys; we certainly didn't want the press advertising the fact that they were with us, as we were very

Little Mal.

much afraid that some reprisals might be made on the donkeys or, indeed, that they could possibly be stolen. They were split into small groups at Slade House Farm, and they were not given collars, so that they could not be identified.

Two of the donkeys were heavily in foal, and both produced delightful offspring. Ellen gave birth to a little colt, which we named Mal, and Penny gave birth to Fiona. Unfortunately, due to the terrible time the mares had experienced during their pregnancies, both foals needed special care, and perhaps this is the reason that little Mal has become one of our naughtiest donkeys! There was always the fear that we might have to send the donkeys back if Mr Gardner wasn't found guilty but, thankfully, at a court case he was sentenced to three months' imprisonment and banned from keeping animals for thirty years after he admitted causing suffering to the donkeys.

As Mal grew he began to cause us quite a few problems: he developed a serious chest infection which meant that he had to be taken into our hospital. We are extremely fortunate here in having what must be the most well equipped donkey hospital in the world, with a wonderful operating theatre and preparation room. The donkeys that come in for an operation enter through a side door into what looks like a normal stable. This is deeply padded and it is here that the donkey is quietly anaesthetized ready for its operation. When it lies down, the pallet on which it lies is then attached to an overhead gantry, and the main doors into the operating theatre are then opened up. The donkey, already asleep, is transferred without any further handling onto the operating table, where whatever treatment is required is given by one of our highly skilled veterinary surgeons. Still on its pallet, the donkey is then transferred to the recovery stables at the other end of the building.

Fast asleep - ready for treatment.

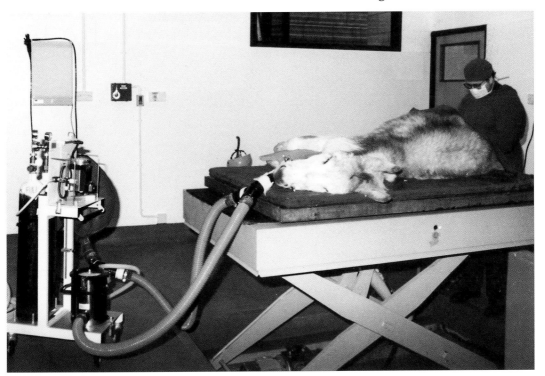

Senior Veterinary Surgeon Andrew Trawford shares his time between the Donkey Sanctuary and work abroad where our charity, The International Donkey Protection Trust, works in many Third World countries. Additional veterinary cover is provided by our excellent local practice, Ikin and Oxenham, and we have three vets almost permanently placed with us, with a further four on call. So the donkeys are never short of veterinary care. This team is backed up by our qualified veterinary

Manager John Pile with some of the group.

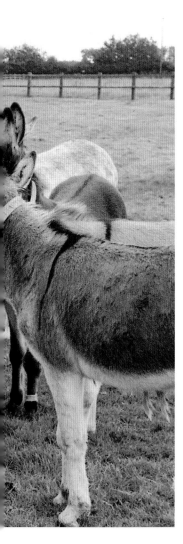

RIGHT ABOVE *Naughty Mal with his prize.*

nurses, and I genuinely feel that if a donkey is ever going to be ill, then this is the best place for it to be! We frequently receive comments from visitors that possibly our 'DHS' (Donkey Health Service) is better than the nation's!

Having recovered from his infection, Mal thoroughly enjoyed the extra care and attention he was receiving. His daily groom was Colette, and she had to be terribly careful when working near him. He absolutely loved the toggles on her coat and, pretending to give her a nuzzle, he would suddenly clamp his little teeth onto a toggle and that was it! He hung on ... and on ... and on! Eventually, Colette's only choice was to undo her coat and slip it off, leaving Mal with it until he had tired of that particular game! Now, as he is getting older, some of Mal's antics have become quite naughty, and one or two staff recently have received a rather harder nip than anticipated, as his little pearly foal's teeth have developed into quite sharp big teeth, and his habit of 'hanging on' has caused our staff to be slightly more stern with him than they have perhaps been in the past.

With Ellen, Mal will soon be fit enough to move into one of the larger groups of donkeys, and no doubt one of the other young geldings will soon teach him a few manners!

Paddy and Crumble: a Lick and a Promise

The aims and objects of the Donkey Sanctuary are quite clear: we are here to take in donkeys or mules that are in distress or in trouble. This sounds clear and simple, but things are not always as easy as they seem, and throughout my years of running the Sanctuary I have been put in a difficult situation on more than one occasion when a donkey has had a companion living with it and we are asked to accept the companion as well – which is for the benefit of the donkey. As you probably know, donkeys create very real bonds, particularly with their own species, but sometimes with a different species, and to separate a donkey from its companion can be very cruel indeed and can lead to such stress that the donkey actually contracts hyperlipaemia, a condition which can end in the death of the donkey and which must be avoided at all costs. The 'companion animal' is usually either a horse or a pony.

My usual problem comes when Charlie Courtney, our Chief Welfare Officer, comes to me with a rather grim face and says, 'One of our Welfare Officers has found a donkey in real trouble, Dr S. He has been abandoned with a companion who is a large retired racehorse. The two are inseparable and apparently they are both in a starved condition and in desperate need of help.' We are not really geared for taking in racehorses, but in situations such as this we have little choice, and so in comes a little donkey with a companion friend far too large to fit in our stables! This is a very real problem for our veterinary department and staff, but in our efforts to keep the two together no time or trouble is spared in bringing them both back to full health as soon as possible. Once recovered, the donkey and horse generally go to Three Gates Farm, where there are already quite a large number of similar cases. Over the years we have found that gradually the donkey and horse drift away from each other and the donkey makes new friends amongst its own species.

Other quite frequent companions to donkeys are goats, and these are amazing. They do indeed form close links with a donkey and it's quite disconcerting on many of our farms to walk into a barn with 150 donkeys happily chewing the dust-free hay at the feeders to find a goat jumping in and out of the feeders at will and climbing on top of anything it can find – even on the back of its companion donkey!

On opening the back of the lorry recently, the isolation unit staff were absolutely astonished when two little Vietnamese pot-bellied pigs hurtled themselves down the ramp. The staff spent an exhausting couple of hours trying to round the pigs up, as they were so full of energy and life and made it as difficult as·

Riding high.

A good place to sleep.

they possibly could! Eventually they were captured, and put in with their companion donkey.

One story in particular, however, sticks in my memory, and this was the case of Paddy. We first heard of this little donkey in November 1992, when our Welfare Officer for Berkshire wrote to say that she had come across an elderly donkey called Paddy, whose owner was going abroad. Apparently, the owner had purchased Paddy more than 28 years before, and he estimated his age to be 40-ish at least. Eunice, our Welfare Officer, was very concerned about Paddy, as she said he was extremely stiff and arthritic, and she asked for a vet to come and see the donkey before he could be sent to us. She suspected that Paddy had arthritis in his neck and back, but as she pointed out, 'Otherwise he is bright and eats all before him.' Her memo telling us about Paddy was followed by a note which caused us a little concern. She said, 'Now he does have a field-friend – a Jersey cow! The owner says that they are very close, and he said the

60

cow would be shot if she was returned to the farmer he bought her from some years ago. I can't say how Paddy will behave, but as I left, Paddy was in his box and the cow was standing outside with her head inside the stable.'

After administering some treatment, the vet was able to issue a certificate allowing Paddy to travel, and in view of the obvious close relationship we decided that Crumble, the cow, must come as well. I can't say how pleased I am that we made this decision, because it was immediately obvious on their arrival that they were indeed inseparable. Crumble is an absolutely beautiful cow, and she is completely devoted to Paddy. She quickly endeared herself to all the staff in the isolation unit, particularly Wurzel, who is in charge of the unit and had looked after cows all his life.

It wasn't very long after their arrival that Wurzel rang me in my office. 'Dr S,' he said, 'do come and watch Paddy and Crumble. I'm sure you will be delighted at what you see.' I left the office for a very welcome break to see what was causing Wurzel so much excitement. Not only Wurzel but all his staff were leaning on the railings watching Paddy and Crumble who, for the first time, had been let out into one of the fields set aside for those donkeys completing their period of isolation. I don't know how long Crumble had been licking Paddy before I arrived, but there Paddy stood with an idyllic expression on his face and

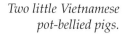

Two little Vietnamese pot-bellied pigs.

61

Crumble was licking him from head to foot. For Paddy this was even better than the mutual grooming that we frequently observe among our donkeys! Crumble's long tongue rasped up and down Paddy's neck and legs and along his spine, causing Paddy to shiver with delight and appreciation. We were all quite fascinated, and I couldn't resist the opportunity to walk in to say hello to both of them. Having patted Crumble I bent over to give Paddy a cuddle, when to my surprise, and to the delight of all those watching, I suddenly felt a strange pressure on the back of my neck which slowly worked its way around to my ear. It was almost like having one of the donkeys' tooth rasps rubbed against me, or perhaps sandpaper with a slightly damp surface! Dodging quickly and looking around, I saw Crumble with what can only be described as a 'happy cow' expression on her face!

The licking ritual seems to take place every morning and, as Wurzel said, the heavier the dew the longer the lick. Apparently Crumble ensures that Paddy receives the equivalent of, perhaps, a spin or tumble-dry!

It soon became apparent that grooming Paddy was not enough for Crumble; when a group of eight small donkeys were turned into the next field, separated by one of our wooden stock fences, Crumble immediately went over to the fence and started licking the donkeys on the other side! Paddy didn't seem all that impressed at Crumble's new menu, but with his strangely angled arthritic neck he managed to get his head through the rails and there to give him a lick was another friend! Betty Doris had been brought over from Ireland and had, until then, been a 'loner'. She was an elderly mare aged 31 years, extremely quiet and gentle and seemed to dislike other donkeys around her. Now, despite being loved by Crumble, Paddy had found a new friend of his own species.

Day after day the staff watched as Crumble licked the other seven donkeys, and Paddy and Betty Doris exchanged nuzzles and stood together as closely as they could with the fence between them. When the time came for the eight donkeys to move on, Wurzel realized how heart-broken the two donkeys would be to part. Both Paddy and Crumble had to stay permanently in the isolation unit, as Crumble's dimensions would not fit comfortably into the normal donkey winter stables, and so

Beautiful Crumble.

when the isolation period was over Wurzel gently led Betty Doris round to where Paddy and Crumble were standing, and to his absolute delight, the two donkeys moved together, and to this day have refused to be separated. Whilst Paddy still spends a lot of time with Crumble, Betty Doris has no time for the cow at all, and has steadfastly refused the morning licking ritual, walking very firmly round to the other side of Paddy when Crumble approaches.

These three companions will now stay together for the rest of their natural lives. Both the donkeys are elderly, but we have had donkeys here who have lived to over fifty years of age, and

TOP *A lick in time.*
BELOW *Togetherness.*

so we are very hopeful that they will have many more years together. How long Crumble will live, I'm not sure. I don't think many people have had the opportunity to keep a cow for its natural lifespan, but I can assure you that at the moment she is doing extremely well and thoroughly enjoying her life with the donkeys in Devon. I am told that she has a calming influence on many of the donkeys that arrive in the isolation unit, perhaps frightened by years of neglect and the change of scene. Possibly many of these have been situated on or near farms and Crumble has played no small part in helping in their rehabilitation to a happier life.

Cyril and Jack: Deliverance from Market

I hate markets. I have always hated them ever since the day I attended Exeter market for the very first time in 1970 and saw seven little donkeys crammed in a pen. In those days I was naive enough to believe that any donkey sent to a registered market always had to go through the auction ring. I learned on that day that, to the donkey's cost, this was not so, and I was unable to rescue those poor little animals who were fated to work on a beach although in a terrible and shocking state.

Since that very first market I have had the misfortune to visit many, many more, and my Welfare Officers and RSPCA Inspectors and other welfare organizations attend specifically to watch for sights which can bring tears to our eyes but which we are often helpless to prevent. In the early days we would occasionally buy a donkey from a market and although this helped the particular donkeys being rescued, we were soon to realize that it could cause pain and suffering for very many more. I well remember going to a breeder's yard where I was looking at a donkey which had been advertised in the newspapers. I heard noises in the next barn, and whilst the dealer was away answering the telephone, I slipped in and to my horror I found a group of grossly emaciated donkeys standing in dung and filth up to their fetlocks and with no apparent food available. I was so angry that I tackled the dealer when she returned, to be told that these donkeys were being 'slimmed down' for the market so that concerned animal welfare charities would offer a good price for them. This was a very difficult lesson to take in but, along with most of the major animal charities, we have had to adhere to our policy of never buying as a charity to enable the dealers to feel that they have a lucrative market.

Our main problem is that, to prove direct cruelty, the donkey has to be in a dreadful state before we are able to get a veterinary surgeon to sign a certificate and then, with police aid, remove the donkey from the market.

Although many of our markets in the UK are bad, you really cannot compare them with some of the sights we see on our trips overseas. The very worst market we have come across is at San Bernabe in Mexico. We have been campaigning for many years to try to improve the terrible conditions that donkeys and horses suffer in this absolutely appalling market. Nearly all the equines brought there are destined to go for slaughter in an abattoir many miles away. They are driven up to 200 miles crammed into open trucks, with horses, donkeys and mules all together, often biting and kicking each other en route, many being trampled underfoot and either dead or nearly dead on arrival at the market. When the lorries arrive they are reversed up to a bank, and the tail-gate of the lorry is dropped down to form a sort of ramp between the lorry and the bank. However,

Note the broken leg.

Waiting in agony to be sold.

A terrible way to load.

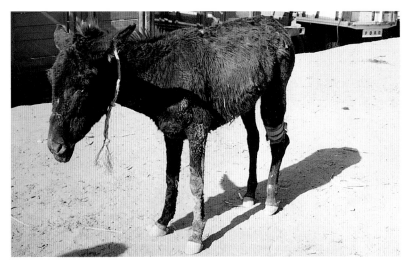

Distress and despair.

Using the ramps we provided for easier loading.

frequently there is a large gap between the two, down which the animals' legs are prone to slip. These poor animals are then hauled back up onto the bank, often with legs broken as a result of this cruel and unnecessary torture. Those that are still alive are herded into groups and sold. Those in too severe a condition to sell are herded into another area, but even these poor animals generally go to certain unscrupulous slaughtermen who are not averse to re-loading them, with broken bones and compound fractures, back onto the lorries in the same appalling way.

Conditions have improved very slightly at San Bernabe since our charity has been working in Mexico. Together with The International League for the Protection of Horses, whom we introduced into Mexico some years ago when we realized we were seeing as many horses with problems as donkeys, we have managed to improve conditions somewhat. The first most important step was to get the authorities to allow our veterinary

69

surgeons into the area, and the second was to persuade owners to allow the veterinary team to put down those horses and donkeys suffering compound fractures and terrible injuries before they were transported to their final, terrible destination. The third improvement was the funding by both charities of ramps which could be extended from the bank onto the back of the lorry, allowing the equines a simple, straight walk onto the sales area. Unfortunately the local people frequently find it too much trouble to wheel these ramps to the lorries, and on many occasions they still use the same inhumane method of unloading their cargoes. I think we have now managed to publicize the awful events at San Bernabe so much that, at long last, the government has taken interest. Dr Aline de Aluja, who is in charge of our Mexican project, has been able to speak with government officials, the Governor of Mexico State has taken an interest, and at long last improvements are beginning to be made in this market.

We find conditions slightly better in other countries we visit. In Egypt, for example, the majority of donkeys in the markets are not for sale. They are waiting while their owners sell the heavy goods the donkeys have transported into the market.

Markets in Kenya are also very varied. Some of the tribes, such as the Masai, are extremely good with their donkeys, which appear to be healthy, whilst others, particularly in areas surrounding Nairobi, do not appear to think that the donkeys have any feelings. These donkeys are very badly treated. We work in close co-operation with the Kenya Society for the Prevention of Cruelty to Animals (KSPCA) in these areas, and provide funding, as they have marvellous contacts and excellent staff who are already doing much of the 'donkey work'.

I think I feel more sorry for the donkeys in Ethiopia than anywhere else in the world. Unfortunately the Ethiopian ass is a very small and fairly fine-boned animal. The combination of this physique and the enormous loads they have to carry, sometimes thirty or forty miles a day, makes you feel that these donkeys, more than any others, all under-fed and under-nourished, are the most over-worked. Again, one can only feel sympathy with their owners who themselves are struggling against a similar desperate fate. Our clinics in all these countries have given a ray of hope to both animals and owners, and

Cyril in the market.

our newest project in Ethiopia, funded by ourselves and run by the Faculty of Veterinary Medicine at Debre Zeit, part of Addis Ababa University, is already helping, not only by providing free treatment and drugs for the donkeys but also by educating owners, which we hope will stand both animals and owners in good stead.

Back in the UK markets, however, which never seem so bad on my return from visits overseas, a lot of supervision is required, and it takes all our time and that of the RSPCA and other animal welfare charities to ensure that they continue to improve. In Cyril's case, he was actually brought into the auctioneer's ring for sale, but the auctioneer noticed that he was breathing rapidly and was obviously very ill. The RSPCA was called, who in turn contacted our Welfare Officer. Cyril was inspected by a veterinary surgeon, who confirmed that the donkey was not fit to travel, as it was suspected he had pneumonia. Working together, our Welfare Officer and the RSPCA Market Inspector made Cyril comfortable in a cow stall at the auction rooms, and the veterinary surgeon started his treatment to improve the donkey's breathing.

Cyril and his new friend Jack.

It was decided to leave the donkey there for a few days while the medication had time to work. The RSPCA Officer, who lived nearby, visited him frequently but, despite all the vet's help, Cyril's condition deteriorated, and the veterinary surgeon said that if his condition did not improve he would have to be put down the next day. However, Cyril improved slightly overnight and the vet was able to confirm that he would be fit to travel as far as Buxton, to our special holding base at Newton Farm. Ray Mutter travelled to Beeston on June 20th, 1994, and collected this little donkey. The worming treatment, antibiotics and the ventipulmin to help his breathing had begun to take effect and Cyril travelled very well, without becoming too distressed. Immediately upon his arrival the vet from the local veterinary centre examined him, and, whilst hearing some lung noises, he found his heart to be strong. The vet decided that, provided Cyril was fed well and looked after, he should make a fairly full recovery. Everyone was slightly concerned, however, to find

Cyril full of lice, with many lice eggs already in his hair. He was left for three or four days, given ample opportunity for exercise, rest and good food, and then he was de-loused thoroughly. Of course, during this time he had to be kept apart from the other donkeys, as lice infestation can be very contagious. Ten days later Cyril was able to make the journey to Devon to start his six-week isolation period and be given the chance to make a full recovery. I know you will be pleased to hear that Cyril has made friends with a dear little donkey called Jack, a gelding, who came in as a very shy and timid donkey. Jack was also purchased from a market, by a caring person who then relinquished him to us, as he was in need of special medical care.

Cyril and Jack are now happily settled, and it is a joy to see them both together, so happy and safe. Cyril has been gelded, as stallions are not acceptable at the Sanctuary, not only because of the danger of putting every mare within sight in foal, but also because of the natural stallion tendency to be a boss and a

Cyril giving Mrs Brown a push.

73

bully, and occasionally to become quite aggressive. Even after they have been gelded it can take some time for these aggressive instincts to abate, so after their isolation period Cyril and Jack were moved to the 'Big Boys' group at Brookfield Farm. Some of the donkeys in this group have very sad histories.

Cyril and Jack, having spent some time at Brookfield Farm, were then transferred together to the rehabilitation group, where they proved to be absolutely ideal for re-homing. Eventually, they were chosen to go to a lovely home in Surrey. Their new owners have marvellous facilities, as their house has stabling, grazing and fencing, all in tip-top order.

Mrs Brown, at Cyril and Jack's new home, wrote to me recently to say that Cyril was a 'greedy pig' and totally spoilt! When Mrs Brown has her back to him preparing his food he gives her a push, as if to say 'hurry up for goodness sake'! Cyril and Jack play a lot together, chasing one another around the field and are indeed very fond of each other.

I sincerely hope that the two of them continue to have a very happy life together in their new home, knowing that at all times they have the security of the Sanctuary if they ever need us.

*I*rish *Thomas*

For many years I had been aware of the terrible conditions for donkeys in Ireland. I had heard of a Mr Barrett who was a member of the Irish Society for the Prevention of Cruelty to Animals and who had started a small Sanctuary for donkeys at his home at Liscarroll, County Cork. On a trip to Ireland in 1976 I managed to visit him, and was most impressed with his obvious love and concern for animals. He was worried, as he was having great difficulties in finding the funds to keep his work going. We were able to help him in a small way, and I was extremely grateful to know that someone was doing something for the donkeys in Ireland.

They say that many of the donkeys in the UK today are the descendants of those originally shipped over from Ireland during the 1914-18 war when horses, which had been doing most

A working donkey in the peat bog, Ireland.

Donkeys are still working today.

of the agricultural work on the farms, had been taken overseas to help in the war effort; they were replaced by donkeys who had to take on the tasks of ploughing and carrying goods around the farms. Many donkeys still work in Ireland today. They are mainly used on the peat bogs which are inaccessible to other forms of transport; they are able to struggle through the deep peat carrying enormous loads on their backs. I remember one day questioning an owner of a group of donkeys being forced into these terrible conditions, and already very overloaded. I pointed out that their feet were in urgent need of farriery attention, as they had grown so long that some of them had curled up in the front like Turkish slippers. The owner turned to me with great sympathy in his eyes and said, 'To be sure, lady, if I were to cut their feet down, sure, they'd go up to their knees in the bog. It's the only way they can walk through it.' Not a great deal of comfort for the poor donkey struggling with painful feet.

Unfortunately Mr Barrett Senior died shortly after my visit, but his place was taken by his son, Paddy, who with his wife and children took over the task his father had started. Paddy and his family are the most wonderful people, and I have nothing but admiration for their devotion to the donkeys and for the love and care that they give them. I took more and more interest in the Barretts and the plight of the donkeys in their care, helping to fund them more, until eventually the Sanctuary employed Paddy and his family and took over the financing and administration of the small unit. The project in Liscarroll now runs as one of our farms. It is, however, a farm with a great difference. They have to be much more independent than any of the other farms, as there is so much office work involved and they also organize the re-homing of donkeys suitable to be placed in good homes in their area. In the beginning the facilities there were very basic, but Brian Bagwell, our Deputy Administrator in Sidmouth, who has enormous experience in building work, immediately went over to Ireland, and over the past years new stabling and a new intensive care and veterinary unit have been built.

Thomas found in distress.

This story, however, is about Thomas. Whilst Paul Svendsen was the Assistant Administrator of the Donkey Sanctuary, much

of his time was spent in Ireland, and on this particular occasion, January 27th, 1994, he had just arrived at Liscarroll to give any help that Paddy and his family required. He walked into the office to find Paddy and one of the local gardai (Irish police), called Patrick McEnery, in deep discussion. They were most concerned about a donkey which seemed to be in a very bad way, and the garda was asking Paddy if he could go and see if he could offer any assistance.

As it was already very late they arranged to go out first thing the following morning. The next day dawned with an atrocious gale blowing, and the rain was driving almost horizontally. Fortunately by the time they got to the house and met up with Garda McEnery the weather conditions had improved, although when they were taken to the field where the donkey was located it was heavily waterlogged and, at first, no donkey could be seen. There was no sign of any food in the field, and as the three of them set off across the sodden ground they could just see a brown object lying close to a bramble hedge. As they approached they could see it was a donkey, but it made no effort to stand, although it lifted its head to see who was approaching. On closer examination they found this poor, seven-year-old brown stallion, with his terribly deformed feet stuck out in front of him in the mud, with hooves so long that it was obvious it would be extremely painful for him to stand. He was in a most pathetic state. It took the three of them to lift the donkey, and they had to get him to walk across the field. There was a terrible wound on his back which at first everyone thought was probably caused by attacks by crows, but they later learned that this was the result of loads being tied on to him for days on end without being removed, causing very bad injuries which had ulcerated and which must have been extremely painful.

For the next two hours the team desperately attempted to make contact with the owner, but were unable to trace anyone. In the field they found a derelict shelter which had possibly housed Thomas at some time. They called in the local veterinary surgeon, who examined the donkey, and it was agreed to try and walk him very, very slowly towards the horse box which Paddy had brought to the end of the road. Although the distance was only about 300 yards, the donkey was obviously in agony, and the team were extremely upset by the time they

Thomas's dreams begin to come true.

reached the horse box. There was, however, no alternative, and with veterinary approval the donkey was carefully loaded and was slowly driven back to the Sanctuary. Garda McEnery, the veterinary surgeon, Paddy and Paul all agreed that if the donkey had not been moved he would have died.

On arrival at the Sanctuary, Thomas (as they named him) must have thought all his dreams had come true. Paddy prepared a lovely warm mash for him and, very carefully and with gentle, loving hands, he was helped into his new quarters. Fortunately our farrier was also in Ireland at that time, and once Thomas had spent a night settling down, Robin started the difficult task of trying to bring his hooves back into shape. It was quite obvious that Thomas appreciated all the attention, and the difference in him after his feet had been pared was quite miraculous. His

LEFT *Standing comfortably at last, he thinks he is in heaven.*

wounds were treated, he was given antibiotics to prevent further ulceration and treated for worms.

After a few weeks in intensive care Thomas was, for the first time, able to be taken out into one of the fields and, with the help of Helen, Paddy's daughter, he was introduced to some new donkey friends. There was no doubt that he was now a very happy donkey, but at this stage a real worry reared its ugly head. Paddy heard that Thomas's owner had been to the gardai, demanding that the donkey be returned to him. Knowing of Thomas's previous condition, the gardai, whilst being very polite, told the owner that there was no way they would return the donkey to him and informed him that they had, in fact, initiated court proceedings against him. With the prosecution pending, Paddy spent many nights worried that Thomas might have to be returned to his owner if the case was not proved. However on July 21st, 1994, I received a message from Paddy as follows:

Happy faces at the Irish Opening.

'I am glad to inform you that we were successful in our court case against the owner of Thomas for cruelty. Judge Mary O'Halloran in Kilmallock Court fined the owner 125 punts plus a donation of 100 punts to be paid to The Donkey Sanctuary at Liscarroll. The judge also ordered that the donkey became the property of The Donkey Sanctuary for the rest of his life. We are delighted with the verdict, and hope that this will be a deterrent to everyone not to be cruel to their donkeys.

Signed: Paddy Barrett, Manager of The Donkey Sanctuary, Liscarroll.'

In November 1994 I had the great honour of going over to Ireland with Brian Bagwell, to officially open the new facilities there. It was an absolutely wonderful day; a triumph for Paddy and his family, and for all the donkeys, including

Thomas, that were there to greet us. The day was further enhanced by the fact that the Chairman of East Devon District Council, Ted Pinney, came with us to Ireland, complete with his marvellous chain of office, and with a beautifully scripted certificate to give to the Mayor and Mayoress of Cork. Speeches were made by Mr Pinney, the Mayor and the Chairperson of Cork County Council, and the final opening ceremony was completed by Father O'Donovan and Father Twohig P.P., who blessed the new building and the Sanctuary in general. Following the ceremony everyone was able to walk around and see the donkeys and, of course, the Irish held a party! The press turned out in force, the Sanctuary was featured on television and Paddy gave radio broadcasts for the next few days, as the Sanctuary has now become a very newsworthy item. As in England, we have a team of Welfare Officers in Ireland, who follow up cases of cruelty and check out proposed new homes. The Welfare Officers were all present at the ceremony and this enabled Sarah Bagwell (Brian's daughter), who helps with the day-to-day running of the Irish Sanctuary, to hold one of the biannual meetings.

Although the buildings have been extended, the Sanctuary only has land available to take up to a maximum of 75 donkeys, with the result that when this number is reached, and the donkeys cannot be re-homed in Ireland, groups of up to eight donkeys at a time are brought over in our lorry to Devon. All the donkeys coming over have had treatment and are completely fit to travel before they leave County Cork. Obviously pregnant mares mean two mouths to feed in the future rather than one at Liscarroll, and, provided the mare is not too heavily in foal, they are the first choice for selection to come to the UK. All the donkeys' names are suffixed by 'Eire' on their collars, and it's nice to see little groups of 'Eire' donkeys staying together on one of our farms. I often think that the winter weather here in the West Country is very similar to that in Ireland; being on the coast we seem to have many days of sea mist and light rain but fortunately, as in Ireland, the climate in Devon is relatively mild. For Thomas, however, the future is definitely in Ireland. Paddy and his family could never let him go now, and Thomas's travelling days are over – just peace and contentment lie ahead.

*T*om Harrison: *a Non-Smoking, Non-Drinking Donkey*

Fat Tom.

Tom Harrison is probably the most well behaved donkey in the whole of the Sanctuary! He came to us in 1989. Since I started the Sanctuary with my first donkey in 1968 I have had so many interesting people doing the 'donkey work' that sometimes I find it difficult to remember them all, but two people do stand out very clearly in my mind. The first one is Brian Bicknell, a Chief Inspector for the RSPCA and his wife, Anna Harrison, who is a qualified veterinary surgeon. I have known Brian for

Promoted to Slade Centre.

many years but was highly delighted when he visited the Sanctuary one day and brought his wife, Anna, along with him. It's rare to meet a couple with such a dedicated, genuine interest in donkeys and I was really impressed with both of them. Before I had completed the excellent veterinary arrangements that we have today I was often in a great deal of trouble when my vet was away on holiday or on business and Anna helped me out on a number of occasions. She was so good with the animals – kind and gentle and yet very efficient. When Brian and Anna offered to help us for a while as voluntary workers in Ireland this was a great help, particularly to Paddy and

84

his family, who were trying to get on their feet and to cope with the many problems they had. This voluntary veterinary help was just what they needed. Apart from helping us in Ireland, every time Anna and Brian go away from home it has been to help animals. Holidays in Greece, Antigua and other parts of the world have always included practical help and advice to donkey owners wherever they may be. It was in fact through Anna that Tom Harrison came into the Sanctuary.

Anna had been aware for some time of this donkey in trouble. Tom was living with some cattle, his feet were growing very long and he was obviously unhappy. Eventually Anna managed to buy Tom from his owner, and then signed him into our care. Tom's only companions in the past had been the cattle and he seemed quite disconcerted by the large number of donkeys that greeted him. He was unfortunately very overweight, almost obese, having enjoyed himself on the liberal amounts of food necessary for a herd of dairy cows. When he arrived, he was nearly six years old, and after two years with us it was obvious that he enjoyed the company of humans rather more than donkeys and so, tentatively, I suggested that the Slade

The best behaved donkey in the Sanctuary.

Centre staff might like to try him out to see if he enjoyed working with children.

I have always loved children; I trained and qualified as a teacher, and during training I took a great interest in those less fortunate children who had special needs. It was in 1975 that I was first able to achieve another of my dreams: as well as giving donkeys love and security for the rest of their lives, I also wanted to bring some pleasure to these children and to teach them new skills. I decided to form a separate charity, as the objects of the Donkey Sanctuary did not extend to funding work with children, and so the Slade Centre was started. After a great many planning problems we finally succeeded in opening an indoor riding centre here at Sidmouth. The pleasure I gain from seeing these children ride and love the donkeys is immense. Qualified staff help the children to learn skills that many thought were impossible, and the real pleasure enjoyed by a child stroking and cuddling a donkey – and the gentleness of the donkey nuzzling the child – is apparent for all to see. It is hard to believe that in view of the thousands and thousands of rides that we have now given and of the thousands of children who have gone amongst the donkeys, stroking and cuddling them, and, sometimes – dare I say it – pinching the donkeys slightly when their little hands have gripped too tightly, never, never has a donkey bitten or kicked a child. There is a tremendous rapport between the two, and the donkeys thoroughly enjoy their time working with the children.

The donkey's intelligence is proved by the way it helps its little rider during the games played and exercises undertaken. You may have already heard the story of Alfred, one of our earliest donkeys, who actually assisted a child in the 'posting' game. Along the side of the arena are placed bundles of cards, and as the donkey and child pass by, the child has to reach over and pick up a card. The donkey then continues around the arena, and the child puts the card in the 'post-box'. The poor child on Alfred's back tried three times to pick up a card without success, and Alfred was obviously aware that his rider was having problems. On the fourth attempt, Alfred stopped, looked back at his rider who was desperately trying to reach for a card. Alfred picked up the card in his mouth, continued to walk around the arena, and stopped right by the letter-box! This marvellous

I love you.

co-operation between rider and child was witnessed, not only by the head teacher of the visiting school, but by parents and our staff who were also in the arena at the time. On many other occasions the donkeys have shown their great rapport; stopping when they feel a child is not sitting comfortably in the saddle, stopping when, on walks along our country lanes, they hear a large vehicle approaching, and going to greet the children as they arrive with brays of delight, which I must say often receives a mixed reaction from their would-be riders!

Learning new skills, and enjoying the 'posting game'.

Riding in the new arena in Sutton Park.

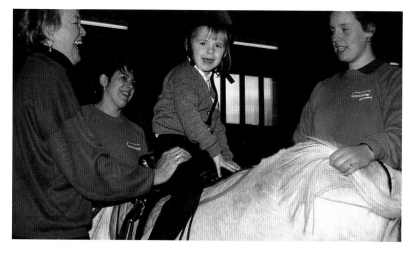

A surprising situation.

Julie Courtney, Principal of the Slade Centre, told me of one little boy who can only say a few words. The moment he enters the centre his face lights up and he beams with delight as he makes straight for the donkeys. He is always the first to ask for a ride and laughs out loud with delight as he is lifted onto the donkey's back. He has already mastered the rudiments of basic riding, and this is his greatest achievement in his young life. While he is so happy and alert the staff are able to work on his speech, which comes more readily with enthusiasm and, as long as he knows he can have another ride after lunch, he doesn't stop talking!

With the Slade Centre being such a great success I was determined to try to open a similar centre in a major city in the UK. As the Slade Centre charity was restricted to working in the Sidmouth area, a new charity, the Elisabeth Svendsen Trust for Children and Donkeys, had to be formed. After a wonderfully generous donation from the Elise Pilkington Trust, the first centre was eventually built in Sutton Park, near Birmingham, and opened in 1994. This means that an enormous number of children with special needs in the Birmingham area can benefit from the facilities previously only enjoyed in Sidmouth. The centre has been an enormous success but, of course, once the initial funding for the building work was received, the running costs have to be considered, and these are quite extensive. Everyone knows the cost of heating, lighting, and other day-to-day expenses, and we have to employ qualified staff for this difficult job, although these are backed up by a wonderful team of dedicated volunteers who live locally.

We had often thought of an 'adopt-a-donkey' scheme for the Donkey Sanctuary, although I resisted this over the years as it seemed rather impractical for our thousands of supporters to have a donkey they feel is their own. We have to do what we consider to be the best for the donkey; sometimes it is better if a don-

The joys of driving for heavier children.

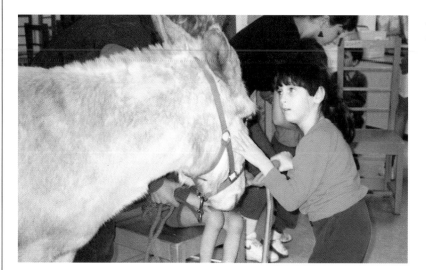

Donkeys enjoy the classroom too.

key stays at Slade House Farm, where he can have special medical facilities close at hand, and on other occasions it is better if a donkey goes to one of our outlying farms, all of which are geared to cater for different types of donkeys. With the enormous number of donkeys we have, and our nine farms, we have always felt that if, say, little Nellie were to be 'adopted' this would, in fact, restrict her freedom of movement. The 'foster parents' would wish to visit her at Slade House Farm, while we might feel that she would be better at one of our outlying farms with her friends or a group she was suitable to be with, or that she might even be suitable for rehabilitation.

With the Slade Centre and the Elisabeth Svendsen Trust, however, the donkeys are allocated to their jobs, have settled down and are enjoying themselves. It seemed possible, therefore, that people could adopt donkeys from these two groups and the funds raised in this way would help with the running costs on an annual basis. One of the donkeys selected from the Slade Centre group was Tom Harrison, by now an extremely valued member of the team. Not only can Tom be relied on to take the most nervous child and instil confidence, he has become used to being driven in one of our delightful little traps. These are used for children who have either grown too big actually to ride the donkeys, as we adhere strictly to an eight-stone limit, or for children who are so severely handicapped that they are unable to sit on the donkey. These children get great pleasure from driving round our country lanes, feeling they are in charge of the trap. The reins are not attached directly to the donkey's bit, but to a noseband, so that the donkey is not pulled unnecessarily or worried in any way. The leader at the side has a firm grip on the donkey at all times. Tom, particularly, seemed to thoroughly enjoy being trained to work with the trap. Donkeys selected for this have to be (a) very strong (b) very mild mannered and (c) enjoy themselves, and Tom certainly seemed to enjoy his training.

The training starts off with the donkey handler standing behind the donkey with two ropes, pulling gently to get the donkey used to turning left and right, and to stop on command. The next step is to attach a log to the two pieces of rope so that the donkey gets used to pulling a weight behind him, and then he is put to the trap and, all being well, no more training is required. Donkeys are far easier to train than horses, and seem to respond to commands so much quicker. I still think that the donkey which stops and refuses to go through a large puddle in the road is intelligent, not just stubborn! Donkeys are not very good swimmers and, to a donkey, that puddle in the road could be six feet deep! He really has no way of knowing until

Summer in the park.

someone walks through in front of him, and having seen that it's only hoof height, then there is no problem in getting him to follow.

When I suggested to the staff that perhaps Tom should become one of the donkeys to be offered for 'adoption', asking them if they could give me an update on how he behaved at the Slade Centre, perhaps telling me any amusing moments that Tom had given them, they all looked at me in surprise. They actually told me that they felt that if Tom was a human being, he would be the sort of person who didn't smoke or drink, and that really sums up Tom Harrison!

The 'adoption' programme started just before Christmas 1994, organized by Mal Squance, our Co-ordinator, and one member of our staff, Sue Hudson, was appointed to be in charge of the project. Neither Mal, Sue nor I had any idea of the tremendous number of requests we would receive to adopt one or more of the eight donkeys being offered. It really has been the most marvellous project. Everyone who participates receives a history of the donkey, along with a photograph and a certificate of adoption, and for a fee of £10 a year they become an 'adoptive parent' with an invitation to visit if they can. There is an excellent video available at a cost of £5, showing all eight of the donkeys available for adoption. We also send a 'Did You Know' sheet.

Each year a festival is held at one of the two Centres. On odd years it will be at the Slade Centre here in Sidmouth and Tom will be present, along with the other three Slade Centre adoption donkeys. On even years it will be held in Sutton Park, near Birmingham, giving you the opportunity to meet the EST donkeys. The donkeys offered for adoption are as follows:

SLADE CENTRE DONKEYS:
Tom Harrison
Tom Harrison gives rides to children with special needs here in Sidmouth, Devon, and sometimes pulls a trap. He is a most handsome skewbald gelding born in 1983.

Tom was purchased by a vet from an owner who had let Tom's feet grow very long and really no longer wanted him. Tom was living with cattle and no doubt was lonely without species of his own kind.

Tom arrived at the Sanctuary in 1989 and became the 4,005th donkey to be taken into the Donkey Sanctuary when the vet immediately signed him into our care after purchasing him. Tom is loved by the children and staff alike. He is well behaved, eager to please and handsome as well!

Daniel P

Daniel P is a grey roan gelding, larger than the average donkey in size and personality! Born in 1989, he is the youngster in the team and, as one would expect, is cheeky and often up to tricks. However, he knows when to be good with the children and they adore him for his naughtiness.

Daniel P (No. 5,139) arrived at the Sanctuary in 1992 having come from a good home which bred donkeys. However, the owner was moving and she was worried about Daniel as he had never paired up with her other donkeys, preferring the company of horses instead.

Daniel settled at the Donkey Sanctuary very well. His nature is such that he isn't going to totally conform to the 'norm' but he's kind, loving and full of fun. At present he's being trained to pull a light trap and seems to enjoy every minute of it.

Dominic D

Dominic D is a mushroom grey gelding born in 1987.

Dominic came from a caring home but when his pony companion had to be put down Dominic became lonely. Worried about his future should he be sold and possibly change hands many times, his owners asked the Donkey Sanctuary to take him into care and Dominic was the 5,903rd intake.

Being a fit, strong donkey, Dominic was considered suitable to join the Slade Centre team. He proved ideal and the children love him. He's not always impeccably behaved – much to the delight of the children and the amusement of the staff: on rides around the arena he sometimes walks very slowly, falling behind so that he can then be allowed to trot quickly to catch up with the rest of the ride! All our donkeys wear collars with their name and number on but Dominic regularly disposes of his and most mornings the staff find Dominic minus a collar. Another trick is that at times he will refuse to go into the lorry and appears to be looking at staff in amusement as he realizes the difficulties he is causing! He is indeed a very clever donkey, very lovable and a bit naughty.

Megan

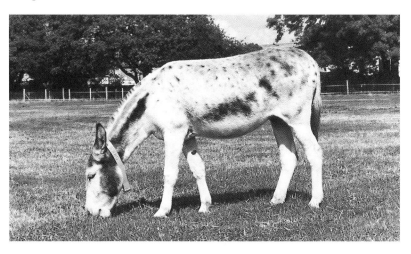

Megan was born in 1984; she is a beautiful dapple grey mare. Megan came into the Sanctuary in 1993 as her owner was terminally ill and wanted Megan in safe hands. We were advised that Megan loved work and goats!

Megan was the 5,888th donkey to arrive at the Donkey Sanctuary. She is extremely ladylike; always well behaved and has proved to be a model Slade Centre donkey. The staff can rely on her to remain calm and patient with the most excitable, noisy child. Megan really is a super, kind donkey.

EST DONKEYS:
Dinky

Dinky is the head of the donkey team giving rides to children with special needs and pulling a light trap at our Elisabeth Svendsen Trust Centre in Sutton Park.

Dinky (No. 1,587) was signed over to the Donkey Sanctuary in 1983 after our Welfare Officer visited his home and found him to have very long hooves. At first Dinky objected violently to having his feet attended to but with perseverance he realized no great harm was going to come to him.

He has a super nature and is totally reliable with the children. He is probably one of the best tempered donkeys ever to be found. Dinky has worked with the children with special needs for several years now, and when a donkey needs to be taken into a classroom to teach children on animal welfare, Dinky is the one who goes because of his impeccable behaviour. He also once accompanied the children to London to visit the Lord Mayor; not many donkeys can boast of that!

Although getting on in years (donkeys can live to 40!), Dinky just adores his work with children. He's also the Supervisor's favourite and she lists as his likes: cups of tea, candy floss, ice cream and strawberry popcorn!

Pascoe

Pascoe is a grey gelding born in 1979 who was taken into the Donkey Sanctuary's care in 1986 when his owners were no longer able to cope and worried about his future should he be

sold. The wife of the household had arthritis in both hands and when her husband became ill she asked for our help. Pascoe was the 2,854th donkey to be taken into our care. He is a sweet little donkey with a very kind temperament and has proved to be ideal working with the children with special needs who regularly visit the Elisabeth Svendsen Trust Centre in Sutton Park.

Pascoe is happy to provide rides or pull a light trap and is much loved by the children and staff.

Donk Dean

Donk Dean (No. 4,774) arrived at the Donkey Sanctuary in 1991. He had belonged to an elderly couple but had proved to be too much of a handful for them. He had been kept as a single donkey and obviously his boredom had resulted in his naughtiness as, once he joined other donkeys at the Sanctuary, he was no problem whatsoever. The staff considered Donk Dean had the right temperament for an EST donkey to work with children, and he has not looked back. Born in 1987, he is the youngest of the donkey group, he is always reliable and excellent with the children. He has grown into a rather debonair, smart, grey donkey, much loved by children and staff alike.

Blacknose Ben

Blacknose Ben is an ex-beach donkey. He was loaned out during the winter months and his temporary owner persuaded the beach operator to sell him to her. Eventually in 1991 Blacknose Ben came to the Sanctuary and his lady owner continues to visit him.

Blacknose Ben (No. 4,781) is a handsome chocolate brown gelding, born in 1976, well suited for his work with the children with special needs at the Elisabeth Svendsen Trust Centre in Sutton Park as he is so good tempered and kind. If the name Blacknose Ben conjures up an image of a pirate then rest assured that he would have the most compassionate personality, as our Blacknose Ben is highly regarded and loved by children and staff alike.